WALKING, FALLING

WALKING, FALLING

Kelwyn Sole

ISBN: 978-0-9870282-8-0
ebook ISBN: 978-1-928476-24-5

Deep South
contact@deepsouth.co.za
www.deepsouth.co.za

Distributed in South Africa by
University of KwaZulu-Natal Press
www.ukznpress.co.za

Distributed worldwide by
African Books Collective
PO Box 721, Oxford, OX1 9EN, UK
www.africanbookscollective.com/publishers/deep-south

Deep South acknowledges the financial assistance of
the Cape Tercentenary Foundation for the production of this book

Cover design: Liz Gowans and Robert Berold
Text design and layout: Liz Gowans

Cover image: Mongezi Ncaphayi 'Come on, now – 2013'
(Monoprint with drypoint)

in memoriam Konstantin Sofianos (1983 – 2015)

Some of these poems have been published previously in: *Canopic Jar, Carapace, Illuminations, New Coin, New Contrast, Poetryarchive, Prague Revue, Punch-In-The-Face Poetry, scrutiny2*.

Quotations from the following sources are acknowledged:
Laurie Anderson *Big Science* (Warner Bros lp OOVVONBE 1982); Aimé Césaire *The Collected Poetry* (Berkeley, University of California Press, 1983); Mahmoud Darwish *Absent Presence* (London: Hesperus, 2010); W.S. Graham *New Collected Poems* (London, Faber & Faber, 2004); Theodore Sturgeon *And Now the News ... Volume XI: The Collected Stories of Theodore Sturgeon* (Berkeley: North Atlantic, 2003); Marina Tsvetaeva *Selected Poems* (New York: Penguin, 1994); W. C. Williams *Collected Poems of William Carlos Williams Vol. II: 1939 – 1962* (New York: New Directions, 2001) C. D. Wright *Cooling Time* (Port Townsend: Copper Canyon, 2005).

Italicised sections of 'Visiting a writer' are from the discussions and correspondence of Marks Rammitloa (Modikwe Dikobe) with the author.

Contents

I

II

III

IV

V

You're walking. And you don't always realise it, but you're always falling.
With each step you fall forward slightly.
And then catch yourself from falling.
Over and over, you're falling.
And then catching yourself from falling.
And this is how you can be walking and falling at the same time.

– Laurie Anderson

I (Off the map)

What landscape is: not a closed space, not in fact capable of closure. With each survey the corners shift.

— C. D. Wright

Vigil

1

The wind seems a distant plaything
of children, querulous, night-befuddled,
and there are no curtains to hide away
the sweep of a city terrible with souls
stretching in all directions.

What dreams to bring, how can I rest
in a place where a thousand eyes glint
all night long, maddened wasps
around a nest? This prospect is the last
of what God promised me

but I no longer listen to Him.
All I know are rainclouds, always
from the north, always scurrying
closer like refugees. Now
we seem without pause
to be in a winter without
recompense, or end

– mine thrums with the passage
of distant trains and their obscure,
whistled danger;
                rumours vibrating
down two lengths of steel that
cut the workaday world
in two to its end
like knives
           through an apple.

If you tried to touch them
in this cold, they would take
the skin right off your fingers.

There are voices all around
stroking politely, so politely –
although they call me friend,
they can give me no true name –

    2

the wind howls
                my sight
tears in need of the horizons
I have lost; I imagine flocks
of birds named for no species
in agitation all around me

like an angry mongrel, or
like desire that's been defeated
by its ending, my hopes
bristle
        yank their chain
to an utmost reach, end up
boasting back, vowelling
challenges to every being
that passes by

through a silence
that will not flinch.

Even if with level gaze
always having to speak as
of something else. As if
there was no someone,
anywhere...

the words that pass between us
grip dire truths on broken wings.
They flutter from their roosts
to feed on a land made up of
all our bodies once more in thrall,
still bowed down and crippled,

a place where we can't persuade
our one hand to make common
purpose with its other.

I have died many times for this:
talked myself into oblivion until,
piece by piece, my country comes apart
in my hands   skin peeling away
a parchment on which I write
speckled with blood and forgetfulness

because I can know only one house
that is myself to speak from, hoping to sense
the invisible promise of the planet's spin
by which a new day will edge at last
into the world
                    and refuse to be denied.

   3

The tongue where absence dwells
knows its limitations:

so is it enough, the waiting?
To bare the chest to
this unusual winter
as if that were a form of
suffering; legs tucked up,
while people still refuse
to rise up, move, despite
the world's incontrovertible

turning. What imaginings
can dance around a child
                    made of hunger,
or the man with his left hand
on his heart and his right
in his neighbour's pocket?

or the beggar who's silent with sorrow
or the rat screaming in the claws
of a cat's dream, or a young man
sullen with righteous anger
at a history he's never known?
Rusted gutters weep down
the walls of ill-made homes,
the air full of politicians'
fricative scratchings as they chase
after their own tails;

zinc plywood cardboard
from destroyed shacks
blown here by the wind
a fruitless migration
of dead birds piled up
against the walls of mansions...

who is doing the watching here?
And who is being watched?

4

I want to travel the finite
journey of the tongue
to its tip, and tumble off like
the loquacious should, into a world
where men and women struggle
yes let us also cross the river

not knowing the compass points,
despite the crocodile and locust,
avatars of beasts
                    those lackeys
in dark glasses
                    who are enough even

to give crocodiles a better name,
who buy and sell the earth,
to whom lives are mere commodities,
who stare at us from black voids
reflecting the sun, then smile,
and nod their heads in greeting,
gift us with words and yet more
words which they shake off
like spittle from the flews
of a dog's pendulous chop.

It's no use thinking of Africa,
or the airport, or even England;
or to trick out a rainbow where
the gold that miners sweat to dig
ends piled up in assenting surrender
like confectionery for your handfuls:

the day will come

when anyone homeless in a mud hut in
prison in a zinc shack will be awake to say:
what are you claiming here, with your skin's
verbiage, with words picked out for you by
the ventriloquists behind facebook or television?

The millstones that grind up virtue
into heaps of poisoned grain
                              give weight only
to the smug pockets of the rich
                              and forgive
greed to invisible, anonymous power

are a weight that hangs off us too,
more cumbersome than our
balls; our breasts; our wallets

while the children of the land
covetous of a new identity,
a tongue that will not be rued
by its owner, that promises
a fresh start
                    are still
fighting in the street for scraps,
or slouching within four walls
with their heads down,
texting.

5

The nails of this night scratch
any face that protests for a dawn:

but a way to act,
in truth? It is, I think, still hidden
somewhere beside us, its elbow
nudging at our ribs, a bemused
expression on its face.

Vleiside

bladder crickets
                  void
their tiny bowels
                  of sound
in this retreating
                  night

as a scalped moon
                  dying on its back
sluices light from
                  its perennial wound
and will not let us
                  sleep

*   *   *

inch by inch a tin can drowns itself
in brackish water and green slime,
dreaming of what it once held

*   *   *

then the sudden eyes
of gravid toads
cheat darkness

First light

Morning isn't too much of a thing
when all you have to do is
open your eyes.
               An aroma of coffee
broods upon itself, mutters
unseen, in a corner
                  while the sun
utters a first cheeped, tentative note:
a canary freed from a cage.

So don't worry.

               Everything you fear,
everything you hope for, may soon exist.

For the moment, though, your eyes itch
until you rub them; flickering tiny irritations
of light across your vision.

               Or is it just
that the neighbours' gardens catch you
unawares
         with a sudden freckling
                  a chaos

of butterflies?

Domestic

A house that's never still,
nor silent. Each breeze insistent
only in its change of moods.
Who cares if pigeons batter across
the sky or if they settle in, heads cocked,
thinking you a refuge? Sometimes things
will make their own way, sometimes just
get thrown from nowhere to a different
nowhere. And the walls move, the roof
held down in truth by nails and screws
or the weight of birds. An unlikely dirigible,
my house, borne aloft on a pledge
of sun, a stench of wind, a raft of stars...

if you stay here too long with me
it will awaken you sighing and crying
and end your nightly sleep. And, athwart
the slope running from sea to mountain,
navigate you from what you know
so quickly that you will have to take
yourself and tack, and tack, to stay
even remotely who you are.

Here the nerveless seasons wheel
in transports I can't fathom. Rocks
knuckle up on every side, sprawl
shadows from whose refuge
ants make trails desultorily until
underneath my door. You can see
the swift judgments of life and death
repeat throughout these days and nights:

in the garden there's one spider more,
one spider less; and a francolin too verbose
must lead its chick into the ambushes
of cat and peregrine. It's as if everything
on the green stem of this mountain
becomes brain, finds ways to feed
an intricate system of reprisal.

Even so, won't you come again,
be a co-conspirator in my plot
to question the law of gravity?
Let's hang on for dear life:
it's fun, even as we lose.
A house that's never still.
Nor silent.

Give us this day

A crane articulates a yellow arm
              to modify
              crumbled
     art
deco
     (so much steel, dug
     into the eyes)

     even higher
              jettisoning a mussel
it cannot break
              down the cliffs of the air
a gull moans
        only to us
            it seems forlorn
– but no matter –

my hand skirting round your spine
is milk stirred onto coffee.

Let's get beyond, but not go past it,
you say, scratching too close
to your crotch (or mine) and both of us
not yet got over sunburn
              this beach
in summer, parking cars and kids
and squeals of road rage
or bonhomie

        the sea
a constant apiary of light:
wave crests shaken free
like bees that gather honey
from the sun

       a brightness
that makes the sea a thousand pulsing oysters

undresses the mountain in its turn
from its cerements of purple, nitpicks it
to screes of flaked and wrinkling stone.

And always a woman standing in the surf
like now, her best holiday of the year,
Tweede Nuwe Jaar; dress rumpled up
around her thighs by two meaty
dish-discoloured hands.
                  She doesn't look happy,
watching us watch her.

You shrug. *Who cares*
when the world
is slowly being
            baked
under a thickening crust of heat.

Seafront

The future wants to show its blurred, ideal face,
though all the maps where it can materialize
are full of holes. *Here be monsters.* Close by
the tide's fetch lessens, though waves pleat up

and flip the sun's image into a twinkling coinage.
All our boats are out to sea. *Excuse me, Captain!*
Captain? He makes a beeline towards my pity
while his friend upends their shared *papsak*

for a final drop. Young enough to be his daughter,
the teenager who walks after me, crooning a song,
holds out a dusty flail of proteas. She can still smile
yet may not have the best intentions, eyes occluded

into *tik*. Three gym-raddled women break off
their conversation to peer out at our slow passage
above the rims of cappuccinos. Their mouths
open like fish, in unison, then close again

– here there's not much for diversion. Shop windows
no longer reflect who we may want to be: are just
dark caves of clutter. Frayed postcards. Scrimshaw.
T-shirts to proudly proclaim a wearer 'Native'.

On the beach the hulk they burned the dealers out of
rots on the sand. It's too far for any surge to reach
and bottlenecks wait in ambush for bare feet.
A world where opposites blur and coalesce –

on one side of the road a Cuban restaurant and flag,
on the other streamers that proclaim the *sang froid*
of estate agents. Even the afternoon's beclouded:
bladderwrack, and kids in wetsuits bob in a surf

clawing to stay near shore with chilled, white fingers.
To be honest, nothing really shifts or changes.
Loud hunger tears forever at the throats of gulls.
Tourists renew their pilgrimages in summer

while routinely the world falls from us. Who we are
is bitten, from teeth chipped and yellowed that
have nibbled around too many spoons. Each year
it's harder to move past incrustations of habit –

"…but after all" I say to the Congolese professor
now reduced to touting parking spots for tips,
"it should be clear to us that when Fanon says…"
– then I find that he's no longer listening.

Wounding the landscape

Every year
more homes along the mountain
more homes up the mountain

beneath them an abscess perhaps
the earth scratches itself
because the houses are scabs
that won't come off

what more can I tell you
this morning
with these eyes

just that the other direction's
not much better

a lashed beach a sun
that hawks up a metallic sea
shrapnelling vision
                        and persists
fetching further shafts of light
with a crone's crooked stumble
to stack as kindling against
my window

the air's gone
strangely still and dead
                        roses
in gardens bare their teeth
the estuary a long brown straw
of water being sucked
in by the land

cars tiny mirrors
in the distance
glitter   flare
messages no one can understand
the blare of an approaching train
the scream of police sirens

any silence temporary as
that train's momentum

nullified
– more suddenly than you'd think –
        shuddering
with a suicide beneath
its wheels

            and the beauty
of this morning halted
dead
        within its tracks.

II *(Politexts)*

I wait at the end of the world for the travellers-who-will-not-come.

— Aimé Césaire

Apothegms

Parliament

For over a century,

white or (now) black,
they have barked
their nonsense
from the same
                              old
lofty kloof.

Parliamentarians

Point out to them a single tooth
of this country, mussel-wracked,
                              some brown
decayed rock that sticks, say,
out of the wet gums
of Langebaan lagoon

and they'll build a boat
in which everybody
they can seduce
with words

will
        proceed
                      to
                          get
                              wrecked.

Praise poets in parliament

Mr. Hand and his five fingers
are now ruling the country.

The President addresses the People

You are oil for our wheels. Oil them.

What holiday is this, precisely?

Gesticulating from the stages
of vast and echoing stadia...
ag, just leave them there
                    to act out
their carnivals of faith and solidarity.

Iconography

We buried our heroes.
We never buried them deeply enough.

History

Around the corpse of the hero
dance the flies of nostalgia.

Public sphere

When one sits with enemies
who act as friends

only betrayal can result.

White liberals

Stop pretending:
you'll lose your land in any case.

The race card

In a world beset
by black or white
there are no seers,
only converts.

Diversity

We speak in eleven languages.
All of them can be used to lie.

Language

As for the law,
it preens itself in English.

Coda: Saving the planet

– As for me,

I'm going to protect
the environment

by building
a lucrative game lodge.

Content removed

And freedom came...

and we cheered and stood
in long queues
made marks on paper while
jets flew over the podiums but
the speeches were faint in our ears
because we stood at the back
but that mattered not at all
we cheered nevertheless
cheered and cheered again

some went back to their fields
and started to till
because they could no longer wait
did not pause to think to wonder
why the words they heard
seemed dipped in so much syrup

others, went back to their shacks
standing tipsily in yellow grass
creaking and fluttering walls
in a malfeasance of rain
sly natterings of wind began
to talk to grumble just
like a long-suffered relative
but they had patience still
watched their children hunker down
to shit among the rubble ruins
with no knowledge of time spent
no arithmetic except for was it
their own ribs which they counted

but these days the big men chase
after their own words as if
these were soap bubbles, as if
our hopes were frivolous, and could
be treated lightly: and we and they
were merely children playing
harmlessly, in sun

while between them and us
is a line of men in blue, in uniform,
who themselves seem to be looking
over our heads somewhere
at someone else.

Yes. The vultures dress in suits,
step over one another and over us
in their haste for carrion. They describe
a dawn that we shall never see

and the wind shouts and shouts again

but we are silent as the grave

The leader

1

Will the reverential toyi-toyis ever
unstick themselves from this jackal?
Fattened, he will not lose his nature;
merely convince us, sheep, to offer ourselves
up to his incantations more often: one
more time, just one more time...

for we are seeds
scattered, a bafflement
windmilling in the dust,
                              as he
is a gourd, with his hard skin

and we pelt him with our word selves,
our ever useless anger,
knowing he is hardness but never seed,
not like ourselves, as his skin
grows thicker and he balloons always
              bigger, bigger,
                              and we know
if he pops, we will no longer recognise
him in ourselves among all the
explosions, confusions:

the sudden dead children in the grass.

2

There is no way to steal the yeast
of the bread that rises to succour
him and his rats' nest of power,
or to turn his feasts of arrogance
his plunderings of language
into a leaven of compassion.

He keeps on living in his skinscape
of callousness and gluttony, where
the compradors have pitched their obese
wagon
        trying to blind themselves
to themselves, himself to himself,
himself his only motive: the endless,
fawning, encrafted devices of his
self-aggrandisement.

Visiting a writer

in memoriam Marks Rammitloa

The old man, glasses awry, squints against the sun.
His mouth crumples sideways into welcome.
Around him Seabe's long vistas draw out a morning
where the sky flows and shivers like a river
though there's no clouds to bring relief. Rows
of small houses meander up and down slopes
that stretch identically into a haze of distance
and heat. I hear him murmur, as if into the air,
words I can't quite hear

and greet him. Look around to get my bearings.
Near his fence a gang of men in overalls peck the ground
with pickaxes, curse perfunctorily at their lack of purchase
into earth. Corpses of cars slain by rust and stones thrown
through their windscreens by bored children rot,
their wheels in the air
                          like dying warriors.
A group of women shell peas into tin bowls on his stoep
and nibble at each other's conversation.

                                    I have lost
touch with township life. I am scared of the township now.
I admire the country people's patience, he says,
as the slow drift of memory footprints through his thoughts.
Drought has slobbered a film of dust on all his crops:
it's a ten minute walk to the nearest shop
and twenty-five on a scorching road to reach the school
where he now works, aged seventy. As boarding master
they make him sleep apart from his wife and, even worse,
he has little time to write during the close, moonlit hours
– the country has changed. It is losing some
of its goodness. Beer is for sale, no longer
given. A knock on the door can be

disastrous. In the old days a traveller
was relieved to sight a village. Now
we are suspicious of receiving strangers.
Though the huge pot of his grandfathers
still holds his circle of neighbours complete,
the population has increased ninetyfold.
The old order of chieftainship is dying:
team fieldwork is gone for paid labour
the older generation is dead
and I am a stranger to them, since I came
back to lay claim to my parents' holdings.

I am a fox among people.

I had imagined finding congenial company among
teachers, but they are dull and mentally scared.
Teachers and nurses do not talk on anything
to do with the people's welfare. They're scared
that this is politics. I find it as depressing
as I found the city when I first arrived.
His mouth goes dry: perhaps the ink of his pen sounds
like a rivulet as his dreams course through the dark.
At night, a paraffin lamp sputters, throws shadows around him,
as the room fills with a smell of smoke and the slow gyration
of his brain cells around their solitude. Just how was it, again?...
the man who wrote what it was to dance marabi,
who joined the Communists *to feel like a gentleman*
but lived among the crush and chatter of the slumyards
invokes that lost world yet, incessantly, into silence,
with his shadow flickering hugely on the wall behind him.

He shakes his head. He wonders if this is what
it means to write; to search for the word he knows
is there, which will cut him off from safety but also
off from boredom, and bring him what he's seeking.

I can't lay down a pen once this notion
enters my mind.

The new explorers

They fold up the pavements they live on,
tidy them away come morning.

It's mere bad luck, they're told, has brought
such confusion to their lives;

though every effort to help them turns, in time,
into torn, wind-drafted paper,

promises, instructions, or prayers to keep
the faith – it all ends up the same.

As they walk on, a world of glass and steel
ensorcels and surrounds them

so even as they move, they never find an exit.
The humdrum of each day

drags their compelled feet from echo to new echo,
through the screeching

parrot cries of taxis, exhausts cannibalising air
till they can no longer breathe

while every car window they question is wound up
against them and becomes

mere repetition of their features. Sometimes dust,
sometimes rain gusts into

their blinded eyes; or a remorseless sun hard as a pestle
against the mortar of the city.

Clouds are sickled out of the blue and seem to cipher
give up hope, all your hope, now!

... but they trudge on, stalking a means to imagine
that further on there will be a place

with chairs, or solicitude, or water – somewhere
they may find rest, and be reborn.

Consider this

Here everyone lives in genuflection
to themselves, to their masters, or to those
who cover their own carapace with words
to convince all the rest of us of their
woundedness. Hysterics on twitter behead
the sentence, recycling clichés and abuse.
No one here admits we are all ramshackle:
no one admits we are so in love with
the mausoleum of grievance and power that
we wound ourselves. And to help us
the Shining Ones are always with us:
who discover the brightness of a conviction
then roll their words towards us, backwards
like little dung beetles; so if we ceased
to be bedazzled, we'd see only arse.

Quartet

Fear is a business.
               – Theodore Sturgeon

1

Systole and diastole of the tide:
the will is not enough to stop it,
and anger will make itself only
an object of derision, breaking
against a rockstrewn rim of coast.
I dream more deeply with the sea,
the cold fist of my heart clenching
and relaxing, clenching and relaxing,
to come to the shoreline of an open
-ing palm and move beyond
                            to catch
their response as children's faces
gleam in its hands, cupped there
like a brief respite of joy
before their parents call them,
as usual, back to the gravity
of a homeland upon which they
did not ask to be born.

2

Grief rises daily to make new stories
from what our forefathers assure us
is in truth. Racists and gunbearers
they were, so often, even those
not yet in their graves securely
enough for us to lock their different
skins away and forget them...

Fuck you, in all your separate colours:
get off of the ramparts of spite, of ego,
of justification, of fear. Self-importance
is a weed that grows on children's myths
and liars' sandcastles. And fear?

Fear is just a business.

3

To look out for a morning somewhere
that will open without paranoia
hate or pain – all our curses silenced,
the feigned smiles relaxing: guns
and knives fused into a final iron
futility: while under the horizon
the dead mutter no more, seeking
no revenge, no timeworn accounting:

who among us will find the courage
to ululate, call out; to insist that despite
everything we have made there can
always be the maverick lunge
of lapsing bone towards love?

4

Let your mouth gape with wonder
at every tiny miracle.
Let her milk nourish the mother,
as well as the child.
Let the past become an hourglass
we can turn upside down,
so the spilled blood is rendered
back inside the burned
and discarded bodies.

Look at the time:

how long
we've spent

on thoughts of murder!

III *(Secret sight)*

... listen to this flesh.
It is far truer than poems.

— Marina Tsvetaeva

The words of lovers

His are a broken window.
His, a forced lock that now rusts.
His are the ashes that splutter
and rail once their fire is gone out.
They're merely a shout in a quarry.
Are hoarse, henpecked old roosters:
are scabby cats cannot cure
their own craving, remembering
what it was to be stroked.

Her words are a shattering necklace.
They're wings seared off of their moth.
They're a tame dog's last, lonely vigil:
or a bucket once brimming with water
now holed and taunting her thirst. Words
speckled like dandruff on her collar;
or a ball of frayed twine dropped
forgotten like a riddle,
                       to unwind
and unwind
            on the floor.

Words like figs long since fallen,
                       glutted
fly-palaces abandoned to lust…

such words can no longer be spoken.

Ballast

Ready for love
         or whatever else
you keep everything
at a slight distance:
one palm raised
invisibly, somewhere
beyond the eyesight

of those
       who treat desire
as if it were by right
that you should always
gaze into their mirror.

Each day the wind throws
its icy buckets straight
at you.
      So,
        the only way
that you stay anchored
to the earth
       is through
the ballast that you choose
to put within your pockets

– you keep your hair
short and light enough
for flight, nonetheless,
just in case –

but in one lurks
an apple you've merely
half-consumed. In the other
a bunch of keys, heavy enough
so you one day
                    can remember
to grope inside to find them,
take them out, and throw
them, forever, far away.

Your body fills my night

Starless,
but your body fills
my night —

you, with
two scars on your stomach,
two stabs,

two wounds;
when you undress they show
themselves

as screams
relived, commas where your life
once faltered

— two memories
of a knife, the size and shape of
blinding pennies —

in darkness
black as this, they turn to pits
beneath my nails…

I don't know
all your story. But no words can
encompass these:

all I know
is that when your belly bares
its witness

your nakedness
lights up my night. For your body
has its own

two stars.

Sunburn

Hot sun, and your arms enfolding sweat and flowers

though summer as usual must warm snakes and scorpions out of the crannies and perhaps you wake each day from dreams of smoke that forecast fire, do not sit there on your patio

resigned and irresolute —

much of your life has passed while you watched a world into being where your body was lit up only through the weightlessness of a thousand reflections

coaxed from pixels and glass

but there's no need to wear today like clothes freshly laundered. Strip till you own the sun with your skin. Feel it enflame the wings of your shoulder blades; let light bloom down your thigh. Pain is tomorrow's journey. Time can unwind you like a spool

and will, for ever, if you let it.

Too much stone: there's stone where you live! When you have green acres elsewhere to drowse in, and the sound of breakers being flayed on hard predestined shores is somewhere beyond your caring.

Hot sun. Hot sun on your skin.

The body is a room

Days the heart stutters to bear
where I have been a lodger, with feet
that have no bearing of their own.

Just a name sweated out in sleep;
relentless, dripping tap of the hours
unsolaced beneath my window.

It's hard to touch when life has been
a recoil from a gun and memory
grants only that. But my room changes

contours with your body. You smell
of soap and the world. My face
comes into shape between your fingers.

    *   *   *

A sky and a field beyond the door,
ajar. At a first step outside,

without warning, the stones tumble
from where my past was shipwrecked.

Pick them up: pretend they're bread –
if you put one in your mouth, they allow

no words not those of love. Gone
are the days all speech was silence.

    *   *   *

What there is of sun strengthens
on your skin. Sporadically, a breeze
that pants like a dog: the usual

halitosis of summer. Not much
of morning left
                    just a wheedling
wavechoked ocean squirming at our feet.

But each day to this weary landscape
of landowners you've brought your
dark eyes. And the strong grip

of your hands – your hands –
these hands I've learned at last
to pronounce with all my heart.

How to balance

They go outside:
hear one another's footsteps crackle
across dry cadavers of what was grass...

he cannot reveal to her
how the clouds always
darken above him where he is
his eyesight rubbed across
a vista of cruel mountains

hoping the sky may unleash
its immensity for him,
just once

      while she has spent
all her life as if at the centre
of a compass rose
               her world
flattened to a plane, squinting
for a direction that may help her
escape identical horizons
no matter what their bearing

while, creaking like a randy toad,
beneath them the world turns and turns
continues turning
               on its axis
dizzingly,

and they
      fall or
      don't fall
      or fall
      or
try to keep their balance

as the planet falls away
from the sun and

night comes again
                    for them
just passengers
                on
the earth

        — this old boulder
on which   they stand
        flung headlong

across the heavens.

How to be lost

It's easy: just close the eyes tightly;
have faith in the dark.
                    If he stumbles and the skin

hangs off his knees, she can call it useful:
a handkerchief to wipe
                    her eyes. At least

they'll know if each other falls ... somewhere ...
but they're two bewildered blind,
                    so who knows

what they'll meet, in darkness? *(Beloved, found
and lost and found and lost,
                    over and over again)*.

More than a few steps in any one direction
on a world that teaches not to trust
                    will render them

exposed. But perhaps one of them will call,
his hand or hers stretched out,
                    although the other cannot see.

How will they know, till someone risks the touching? *Yes:
but who will be the first, do you think,
                    daring to be wrong?*

To waken

for Rochelle

A booting laptop hems and haws
somewhere in the house,
belches fully to life with
the foretelling of a disaster,
or a filmstar's prodigal
sperm, just fallen,
that will fertilise
merely gossip
           and you yawn,
stumble out of bed

the uncertainty of your singing
floats out from the shower
             as we start
to travel this journey yet again
of waking up,
             a sun like beaten tin
gonging each and every roof
to pulse with fractured fire.

You saunter, wet, into my sight
knuckling the sting out of your eyes:

lifting palms up towards my face,
fingers not quite closed

             I try
through ten brief gates
past flesh and bone
to peer at you and know
you as you are.

All the years yet to come, long
or short as hours already spent,
looking outwards from this house
to some space indistinct
but waited for, our future
tiny as a promise,
huge as all the sky

despite time
ticking like a bomb

the sense that all things slide
back into their place
                    returns

so the shuttered light of understanding
may open, fetch more dawn for us,
penetrate
              beyond your lids
so you can see I am always here,
and ready.
                    And you?

We walk towards the sun.

Secret sight

No streetlights, no moon:
a room gone so black that
your nipple's lost to sight –
yet I stroke it with a thumb,
its lozenge; hear your flesh
stir as your drowsing steers

to a new language. Drifting
in the synapses of a world
that is now shadow, we lie
between dream and dream,
a space where two bodies
are blinded, to become one.

In my life I cannot stare
past your beauty and see
who you are, in light…
meaning: I am awake more
in the dark. Us, here,
almost. Only just. Where

there is no yaysaying,
no lamp's brashness, will
startle me out of finding
you. Touch me I touch
you. At last: the shape
of things is their face.

IV *(Pen/insular)*

In my language, there is seasickness.

– Mahmoud Darwish

Morning Song

The sea

is cold
         but each dawn
touched

with fire

o   grey flecked corpse

feel the sun
at your lips

and   waken.

Autumn

This morning
a yacht, spinnaker puffing,
scratches a silver line
in its wake
with a fingernail keel

and the coots scatter:

as we turn, wind
is an icy frisson
across the face
                    yet
on the shoulder
of the mountain
the debris of spilt
sunlight has begun
to smoulder,
furtively.

How uncertain
is this summer
of its own destiny,
its ability finally
to be lost!

Sailing journal

The sea as metaphor of the sea.

— W.S. Graham

as we left harbour
    a band kept playing
        though not for us
            — us? mainly we hung
                on for dear life

            my trousers
        were drenched
      over and over again
    plus all the cash that
was inside my pockets
    (although i didn't care
        as there was nothing
            remotely near to buy)

            our skipper bore a mop
        of white whiskers also
      a huge pair of sunglasses
i noticed the next day
that both of my tan shoes
    had gone quite chalky
        i guess from all the salt
            but his beard was that way
                even before we left

        we watched shearwaters
      skim aslant the waves
    the wind picked up a note
then another note
              to starboard
a shy albatross tracked us out

for quite a while or maybe
he was following the fish
then a humpback whale
tried to scratch its back
on our keel only to vanish
utterly
pity it didn't breach!
yelled the mouth behind the mop

a yellowtail leaped aboard
gasped and appeared
immoderately surprised
thumped across the deck
mouth gaping wide
ours too were agape
but if confusion reigned
i'm pleased to say
it didn't last too long

we saw death reach out
persuade both of its eyes
finally out of focus

with that one exception
the fish stayed in the sea
likewise with one exception
we stayed where we were as well
(we managed to haul her back
aboard just in the nick of time)

... the rest of the voyage?
　　well, mostly we went up
　and down up and down up
and
　　someone got sick up-
　　　wind (!) we had to duck
　　　　a hotchpotch of spume and vomit

　　　at the time i didn't quite fathom
　　his bleak face his discomfiture
but now suddenly i find writing
　all　　down　　made　　dizzy
　　　this　　has　　me

Kel-wyn

'Keel-lover'

1

              breach
If a whale were to   too close to the boat
in this swell
          he would not see it, so determined is he
to persuade his brain away from seasickness
by staring   at the horizon.
         fixedly

2

Even when overlooked, waters

never to be discounted: time
after time the blinking lids of light
disclosed across its surface coalesce
into a vast gaze of disinterest
not to be returned
with any confidence –
             the sea
does not coddle its children;
                as one,
he hunkers down through squalls,
or trusts to skidding compasses
past sleeting rain and windscream
only to be exiled, again and again,
finally stranded ashore: and comes
to himself walking upon doctrines
merely of rock   or sand.

Garden songbook

A day of birds

Night holds me
in its hot breath stink
as if it were an owl, claws
in front of a mantling
of huge wings which is
all the world I
can see

until I hear

– palpable through
whatever chink exists
in silence – nearby
the hooting of an owl,
unscripted,
unexpected,

just before

the first murmurings
of light

*   *   *

Though the birds have broken
the fast of their silence with clusters
of notes that swell to berry-ripeness,
the dawn still sulks below the horizon,

then breaks

*   *   *

– a morning raucous
with the clangour of a francolin,
sound enough to rub sleep
from your eyes, harsh
and granulated as sand.

   * * *

In the neighbour's yard
chickens grouch and gossip
over old grain

   * * *

Through the half-words squawked
from the open bathroom window
of a newly married couple, frustrations
of a mated pair of humans
are parroted at large.

… Two birds in the hand
aren't worth one in the bush?

   * * *

A flock of waxbills
          arrows
swiftly past my sight
          chips
tiny bubbles of sound
          across
the air that languidly
          drift,
falter down, and then
          – pop! –

   * * *

On the lookout for an opportune nest,
the black cuckoo cannot help but proclaim
its sadness,
          but will still abandon its chick

*   *   *

The earth begins to toast, flattened
to the gaze like bread buttered with
congealing light
          patches of wispy grass
seduced from their shade now hold
no more sustenance than straw.

Somewhere, two car stereos
declare hostilities: butt their heads
together unmusically again
          again
     again
  again:

    from the end
of one long stem
        a tiny prinia flirts its tail,
        ratchets its small contribution
        in response

*   *   *

With each
    tree
that starts to
      fruit
the pile of bird
        shit
on the front
        porch
thickens

*   *   *

A robin finds a clump of *bitterbos*
from which to plagiarise
its neighbours

                    and, through
the sweetness of its copying,
its slightly fudged facsimiles,

bullies the owners of the songs
into quiet

    *   *   *

A mirror that could have chosen
any place at all
to settle and nest a world

has leaned and been forgotten
against the side wall
of a shed rotting in a corner.

For days it has not budged
but simply repeats
the wrong way round everything –

and so disruption. Especially for
the composure of
a thrush that gives up a hopeful

gleaning through fallen leaves
and scuttles up,
flicks his wings in fury, sticks

out his orange *boep* even further
to peck
and clatter at his only rival:

himself

* * *

In the distance
cyclists inch mite-small
along the enormous flank of the mountain,
through its tangled green fur: above them

starlings can't help themselves,
but flute delinquent words

* * *

A brownian motion of swifts
pillages the high heavens

and is gone

* * *

Westering, the sun bruises
its clouds, the sky
                    an aviary
where colours – pink, orange, cerise, violet –
briefly beat frustrated wings

while a claque of roosting guinea fowl
over the back fence
                    rides
the nag of tunelessness
                    to death

* * *

Suave hymns from the steeples –
a muezzin's octaves soar above the domes –

and, in counterpoint,
the cawing solitude of crows —

hoarse.
       hungry.
           watchful

    * * *

My body is becoming
too diffuse for its boundaries:
I'm threatening to turn into
a twist of paper
            shedding meaning,
a dust devil swirling out of shape,
a vast dishevelled tree of birds
full of song and lice and secrets.

Even so
will night slink back to save me,
that sly black cat?

"Poetry, being useless…"

A colloquy of doves somewhere
out of sight
        in gutters
            on pilasters
is enough to drive any hypochondriac
to sleep

those plump breasts coo roocooing the sublime
… perhaps we can make a pie of them.

But somewhere another bird with
a skewed bill holds me prisoner
with its boundless loss of song,
with drab indifferent feathers,
a vexing lack of colour

— even against a background
of prosaic winter bush
desperate for lyric rain
it cannot make a showing

is just a moving outline

appears fitfully to sight
hopping onwards ever on
wards, and still blocks
my eyes which strain
for philanthropic light.

Food disappears off the ground
like magic into its evil crop
of rumour:
        cast-off scraps;
cuttlefish detritus lost from cages;
insects too stupid for avoidance

and I
stumble behind wherever I guess
it leads, truckle to its discordant syrinx,
those disconsolating calls.

Behind this bird
another bird I also cannot see
is waiting. Another behind
that. Another, then another

poised to become a flock
(if they flew off, would anyone be the wiser?)

Maybe I could persuade it to puff
out its chest, strop its beak, cackle,
become some other shape...

then it might help me
start again.

Reading what our children say

They will no longer come into our room
so we are crouched over slightly, from
listening at their keyhole. Their smiles
are enigmatic as they follow the lit beacon
of their friends, with shoulders hunched up
and complicit – each journey that's assayed
turned inward, engrossed as if on pilgrimage
to reach another advent of the word flayed
from its flesh. Singly, they stride the avenues
texting back an answer: the whole world
repeatedly at the tip-ends of their fingers
so long as they don't lift their heads,
to look at it.   A cellphone clears its throat, burps
into life with a facsimile of melody
and draws my daughter into gossip.
She has no sense that, while she fondles
the planet's maunderings, an impediment
may rise up in her path to trip her up: or
her own feet tangle, and lose their way.

The journey

in praise of Roscoe Mitchell

the lemon sound
               of a sax
glares
      from rock, dazzles, over
                    flows –

squeezes new tastes into each ear

      chordtassles like grass
                    commingle
      with the hairs on your nape
                prick up

                   then bend
     in a hearsay
     of cold wind –

there is a place for melody
               somewhere,

but not here!

nonplussed you're
slapbang inside

a hurricane so total, it fills

                   the curvature of space
with rain
      and the whole world drowns

why is there a
$$h \quad i$$
$$w \qquad r$$
$$l \qquad\qquad l$$
o   o   p in my song?

bodyraft frail on tides of rhythm, headhole spiralling down to a drum ...

... and then you're in the clear

                and drifting calm while

      ahead clouds disperse to

        arpeggios of sun

        and a light that

                sings

Poem that tries not to finish

for Tomas Tranströmer

I took your poems into a wilderness
where time was ordered into simple
quotas of mist, sun, wind, dark:
and found a hut, profoundly small,
where it was possible to sit and stay
sitting.

In its room's cracked mirror they grew
first as an image, a mannikin's titles,
then in colours that rose to veil the air
– purple gossamer, mourning sable –
semaphoring towards meaning, still
incomplete:

as pages began to discover letters,
drawn together: nascent phantoms
quietly moulding into words you
had nudged awake to find their will
and fly like birds, gaining muscle,
aflutter,

the single grace notes of your speech
diversified. At last you were a presence,
a body grown piecemeal slowly outward
from your mouth (your hands, the rest
of you upwelling) as if you were a glass
slowly

filled – how you must love wine! –
while you crammed space full of a land
indifferent to my certainties. At home,
surrounded by books, with other voices
competing, I could never hear just
you:

but now the snout of your sayings
grunts and roots me out. You, who
do not fear to wrench the muzzle off
the unimaginable, the not-yet-spoken,
or to claim love from the rent of your
frozen

soil. Your angular gift; who knows
the fiercest disrespect is to fill poems
with the violence of completion, or
summon them to serve the trumpery
of the easily flattered mouth or
ear.

No. Clear vision is not to salve
those who allow the fornications
of dogma to scuttle on their skins:
it is the brutal heart of loneliness
insomniacs find, transfixed in
cold

moonlight while the train's asleep;
or the body spinning past control
with fear as the car skids across
a road of ice, and you recognise
death's looming headlights flash
closer –

it is a bloodhound when it starts
to be transfixed by the faintest whiff
of truth; a dream of singing which
turns to song; a gentle touch of
roulades on the keyboard; all
this,

all life's steaming entrails must be
sorted through and named. I stop
reading, only to find the gimlet of
your hunter's gaze on me yet. You
say: enough. And silence bites
my tongue.

My garden at night

shrugs, and changes its dimensions.

I go to bed to the sight
of luxuriating grass dappled by shadow,
but in the morning? Stones:
stones: stones

that deliver themselves
                like letters from the mountain,
each bearing underneath
                a unique version
of a scorpion seal
                and come in darkness
        more persistent than the sea,
the waves that brag vainly in the distance...

blushing in oranges and reds
from oxide and from lichen
                the smaller ones
that seem to creep overnight
across the lawn, waylaying
good sense
          will one day
              be enough to bury
all four walls in which I cower.

    2

Even worse, to learn
that larger rocks can sing. Yes:
in an eerie, painstaking monotone
so low, only the forsaken
or mad have fortitude enough
to hear them

yet
their droning is the only thing
that stops our planet cleaving:
prevents its halves
                    flying outwards
into space, half-apples
                    split from their core

and we're kept sane by this,
alone: otherwise we'd twin
into opposing mirrors, fake faces
            that goggle at each other,
each claiming love
for what, in truth, is
just a copy
            of itself.

   3

Sometimes, pushed
by one nor'west squall too many,
or a puffadder's bad breath, or by
the negligent forefoot of a spider,
a chunk of the sandstone is coerced
into letting go — only for a second —
its grip. It is enough

O relax its grip O
O to tumble down to where I stand
please no O where I
live

and a car is crushed,
or a flock of guineafowl,
or *gogo*'s laundry room
plus the pastor's swimming pool,
obliterating his niece and nephew
and curtailing her spin cycle…

So dawn's no abstract beauty,
here. Rocks stand still at last.
Breezes shift within their journeys,
guineafowl eggs begin to stir,
and everyone starts to breathe
more normally again, as if it all
were over.

But no. The opposite
of avuncular, half-arsed,
biting my lip at the foot of
an unplacated mountain,
where rocks can dirge then
lose their grip, to plummet
into smithereens

among the washing machines sun screen
pristine plunge pools down below
here where I am

I must have faith
that my own disasters
will be small and incremental —

that's why I drink my coffee
in the backyard every morning,
apparently at ease
                        but hypnotized,
gazing up the slope as if
enraptured by its tiers
of aloes, bushes, flowers…

though with one eye
truly
        on the stones.

Concerning religion

In late afternoon the soul,
if you are not careful, may
begin to lounge
                and pool away,
like a shadow welling from
your body, further and further,
until it brushes the horizon
to then take flight
                        — the light
flinching on a distant window
can catch just a splinter of it
in passing, and spark,
for a second
                as a rumour
that flames
                out —
                        but that
is all there is.
                Though you
would supplicate it into shapes
more tangible
                with prayers,
or threats,
                or conjugations:

that is all there is. Now
may we attend to something else?

Old toppie

Despite his hair-shirt dreams,
the breaths of the sick man
rustle like silk. Water
glinting in a glass
at his bedside
          the way sunlight may come to light
up the sea, rocking at
its least motion –
the sea is always tipsy. He knows
everything in the world now
finds a path to wobble
away from him;
          wears his face
like an eroded mountain,
a history of words tumbled
into a scree at its bottom,

his mind drying out, though his palate
feels furred with moss –
a carpet, long-dampened,
heavy, kept in
          a sunless room.

This is the time
of life when nothing will ever
yield again: he's
          become a disordered
carnival, his cells staggering, cavorting
like drunks
          revellers no
longer with a path, fit only
to vomit out the letters
of his name

– yet around his bones his flesh refuses
to unfurl, and flower, into death –

a footfall. A cough. He still
does not know who,
                          this time,
will be coming.

Second chance

for Natalie Bruiners

With two hips of titanium
and a spineful of screws,
and the scar of appendectomy
plus another over the colon,
and a sliver of bone somewhere
that still throbs
reamed into a muscle

perhaps it was
                    that somewhere
along the road I forgot to die:

I ladle two pallid flippers
into my shoes every day,
as if these feet
did not belong
to me
        but
                along the path
to death
            perhaps I
was distracted by something –

a stirring in the grass, the tingle
of a breeze kindling across skin,
or the tiny thud made by a seed
as it gave up the ghost
and fell to ground

– whatever it was, its shape is
lost.

        But it was enough.

V   *(Heading out)*

But the sea
                which no one tends
                        is also a garden
when the sun strikes it
                and the waves
                        are wakened.

– William Carlos Williams

Cape Town™

1

A tablecloth has seized
Table Mountain by the nape of the neck:
afternoons of autumn disembark,
strew the rocks with the jetsam of storms,
and suffocate. Distant mountains
chew their horizons to a haze.

In the reeds of those wetlands
                                    not yet made useful
by an icing of cement the wind buffets,
and bamboo clacks its pincers

— a rivensound —
– a horripilation –

we live here, where the sea keeps
destroying its own posture of repose
offered up to a succession of shorelines,
its full stop ...

in autumn, the south-east wind seems to come
straight off the Antarctic
                                    incessant sands
shift
        so who can stay sure
                                    of anything
terns cry
            as they hone in for a final roosting,
preferring beaches with a shed rubbish
of ever-renewing, fetid seaweed
to the pristine traps we market,
mark out for the tourists —

strings of cars fart
and wind around the mountain, obedient
to the highways some wise man decided
should go nowhere else.
                    Yes. Circling an ocean brink
we drink it in with our eyes, hoping
never to touch bottom.

At night there are those
who still try to crane their heads back
far enough to see the stars they're told
are there, fleeing away from them:
this just means they greet each day
on wobbling knees, can't stand up straight
enough even to be called to mother, to the earth
they're told is theirs by birthright
but on which, in truth, all
of us balance precariously
                    and which always
opens up beyond us still unknown
into abysses of light
                    and vastness.

            From where I stand – the Mountain
            notwithstanding – this continent
            can only point

            towards the north.

    2

I keep no constant station
except myself. No stance at all.
From this chair where I sit,
an ageing, untidy primate
caged in by right angles,
by the grudged space of oxygen
I have built around me,
from suburban grids of streets

and walls and higher walls
behind which I guess at others
who wear their skins for a while
like mine, I come to guess also
at a variant topography

but the credulities will not stop
outside my chinked window,
or the diligent hammers and saws of
neighbours each goddamned weekend,
or that thing that simpers squeezing through
the mirror of the magic box I switch
on at the edge of the room
every evening. Though all of these
– I fear – reflect me.

The Muslims cut down trees
and pave any stubborn lawn they find;
the Christians implore and bustle with
their organs late into the afternoon;
while children knock down nests
and play games with firecrackers
and everywhere, everywhere
there's a smirking zoo of cats.

Every day I'm troubled by
a ghostly insistence of trees
in plenitude, in front of me now only
as paper, my pen poised above a desk's
dead wood

but most of all
the inkling that somewhere
just above my head, above this roof
a huge tree I cannot see towers,
tilting over further with each year
uncertain when to fall,
tap roots delved wishfully
between pipes and patios

into the poor soil; its leaves
clap-clapping their hands at
a margin of clouds where

gulls ply straight lines.

At night something shimmers.
There are voices I never wish to hear
on the other side of the hedge,
over the garden wall where razor wire
artfully mimics vines. There,
meat sizzles, and mosquito zappers
purple the night with the death
of tiny wings, syn-
copations of abrupt extinction

till eventually those voices too
become inarticulate with nostalgia
or drunkenness and fade away

and silence
                hangs again over
the sleepers in their rooms, in their houses;
insinuates a lullaby

of disengagement.

   3

A *tik* house cants peeling pillars
into rain. The tenants everyone
here swears must be Nigerians
are nowhere to be seen, though
a pimply white girl in a tanktop
scuffs her sneakers on the stoep,
snivels without pause
                in her misery
of need

      across the street,
girls' faces yearn in
crepuscular browns and blacks
as they walk past arm in arm
glancing but briefly
               at a sign
that hangs
       – *McDONALDS* –
on the corner
       like bloated tissue
red and overripe
as a diseased heart.

All around
        any sense
of community
has been broken,
invaded:
       the people,
stunned into a rictus
of smiling compliances,
lean into the fretful months
expecting downpours,
expecting the wind
as usual to get even
brisker. For the poor,
building projects sprout
fitfully:
       proliferate
tiny houses the colour
of used tampons, and
suitable as hen's teeth.

There's an old woman
already moved into one,
but as for now we
ignore her: one day
we'll get her out.

Surreptitiously, all
start to eye them
clumped together
in neatened rows
like soldiers waiting
to be dismissed,
wonder how many
banknotes will be
oil enough for entry.
We know very well
a politician's word
is like a die:
              a truth
with six sides,
that changes with
each new circumstance.

Money holds us all
in thrall, a lock
that never rusts —

    4

the power of the rich
who always want things stable,
who always know better,
who sing out their anthems
to markets and the growth rate,
while hiding politely behind
a walled estate, alarm and dog

men and women
with bemired words
on their lips and profit
on their minds

and their soft hands

rap their cold spoons
of commerce once more
against the tepid bowl
of another morning as
the sun licks wearily
across its rim.

The world they build –

laid concrete:
our children's play
cinched in by wire.
On the plot of
an ancient *kramat*
a hotel has risen
up from the dead.
Roads roll out
their hamster's wheel
of miles
        where limousines
with tinted windows
pass by, as if
to keep a secret...

if only someone
would plough this sky,
if only wring
its clouds of water,
drop by drop,
so that the drought
in our hearts
could end, and we
no longer be
immured to a mere
rain of winter
again about to settle
cold upon us –

when will it come,
a winter for our discontent,
amid shopping malls and stadia,
with their circling congregations
of enraptured shacks and houses?

5

Who can speak for us –

you,
walking on a pavement
as you brush the buttons
of your smart phone
until your face lights up,
so that your face lights up?

You
in your darkened lounge
before a laptop's jaws,
agape as the web's shining
screen of connection
through shopping
slowly ingests your face?

You,
who blow your brains
out through the mouth
of a vuvuzela, and make
a flag out of your face,
assiduously counting
the days until the next
dribble of a ball?

You,
who shiver behind
newspapers pinups adverts
plastered over corrugations

of iron and asbestos
as a hopeful wallpaper;
around a home that
leans, bids fair to fall,
half way up a sand dune?

— who can begin to speak,

give us back our touch
to place upon this world?

6

Lost from the vistas
of the heart,
                    worn
away in its tides
of private blood

with every eye
a broken window

what have we become —

a carcinoma of construction,
the Mountain's aquifers bottled
up with concrete so we can
not even drink clean water

we try to step outside
                    our shadows
to see whether there is anything
we are not already braced for
new to fear

as paraffin and flame threaten

to tip towards their union

in a shout of wind

we try to speak
to call
towards
        each other

but all that prospers
is an unvowelled language
minute on every screen
lettersrammedlikeboxcars
upagainsteachother.

Here all stays becalmed,
despite the weather:

shaped roses and hibiscus
bloom in every garden waiting
for the hand of the gardener
to one day lop their heads away,
to be placed inside four walls
then treasured for their beauty.

Lives are spent inside
an echoing hall of mirrors:

in my city
another city sits, trying
its level best to sell itself;

though in that city waits
another, still in the dark,
but not deluded.

    7

Branches start to jangle with
the wind's plectrum.

From your attic framed
by a scaffolding
of alien trees I see
the sea languish,
a vast calm expanse
starting to flag,
and knowing too much

— twilight numbs itself

from a distance
that never seems nearer
that falls unscreaming into night

                      how
I wish

the corrugated plate of the ocean would
shudder, a crack appear where no one sees:
till an enormous wave upwelling from its cause
deep in the secret of the planet would make
seabirds scream and shear above its passage
and only fish and the boats by chance already
riding in deep water would not notice
the wavecaps stir up,
flutter into startled geese...

how I wish
it would draw nearer, that some
would choke in water

and the great stone peninsular
lizard frozen underfoot stir,
shrug the roads off its flanks
and start
          to move
               into the sea.

8

All this. But not to forget

there remains around us a geography of birds

the dumb good luck that we sometimes look up

at the hosannas

of pigeons that rise up with each new dawn

bellies briefly aflicker chording the sun's sigh

as they swirl

the urge we have to glance down into ponds

shining like quicksilver which hide the frogspawn

throbbing beneath

and tiny timid creatures flinch in bushes as we pass

while forever close at hand we hear the undeniable

rumour of the ocean

of breakers flensing rocks, a glare off sea a wavering

of something, darkly trembling, not breaking the surface

that summons the eye

something found but never to be resolved a continent

of water where everything is gloriously not in order

and the spirit lifts

as icy spray puckers the air so it's just as well this city

is nailed down by all its pylons and lampposts or it

would just fly off

there is memory on our side our songs of joy and defiance

that waver but won't be silenced, dreams and wishes that long

to labour unrepentant

on their way from one mouth to the next, and whisper

9

turn your life into a ship –

then turn your ship into this sea –

when can we seek what lies to windward?

Printed in the United States
By Bookmasters